To

Benjamin Howell

God bless you

as you leave us

God bless you

as you start at school

God bless you

all the days of your life

With love from the Noah's Ark Team

Xxx

Summer 2018

Written and compiled by Lois Rock
Illustrations copyright © 2007, 2009, 2010 Sophie Allsopp
This edition copyright © 2016 Lion Hudson IP Limited

The right of Sophie Allsopp to be identified as the illustrator of this work has been asserted by her in accordance with the Copyright, Designs and Patents Act 1988.

Published by Lion Children's Books
an imprint of
Lion Hudson Limited
Wilkinson House, Jordan Hill Business Park,
Banbury Road, Oxford OX2 8DR, England
www.lionhudson.com/lionchildrens

ISBN 978 0 7459 7641 9

First edition 2016

Acknowledgments
Every effort has been made to trace and contact copyright owners for material used in this book. We apologize for any inadvertent omissions or errors.

Unless stated, Bible extracts are taken or adapted from the Good News Bible © 1994 published by the Bible Societies/HarperCollins Publishers Ltd UK, Good News Bible © American Bible Society 1966, 1971, 1976, 1992. Used with permission.

The Scripture quotation on pp. 56–57 is adapted from the Holy Bible, New International Version Anglicised. Copyright © 1979, 1984, 2011 Biblica, formerly International Bible Society. Used by permission of Hodder & Stoughton Ltd, an Hachette UK company. All rights reserved. "NIV" is a registered trademark of Biblica. UK trademark number 1448790.

The Lord's Prayer (on page 55) as it appears in *Common Worship: Services and Prayers for the Church of England* (Church House Publishing, 2000) is copyright © The English Language Liturgical Consultation, 1988 and is reproduced by permission of the publishers.

All unattributed prayers are by Lois Rock, copyright © Lion Hudson IP Limited. The prayers by Mary Joslin and Sophie Piper are copyright © Lion Hudson IP Limited.

A catalogue record for this book is available from the British Library

Printed and bound in China, March 2018, LH54

THE LION BOOK OF

PRAYERS

TO KEEP FOR EVER

WRITTEN AND COMPILED BY LOIS ROCK
ILLUSTRATED BY SOPHIE ALLSOPP

LION
CHILDREN'S

Jesus told his disciples to be faithful in prayer, saying:

"Ask, and you will receive;
seek, and you will find;
knock, and the door will be opened to you.

"For everyone who asks will receive,
and anyone who seeks will find,
and the door will be opened to those who knock.

"Your Father in heaven will give good things to those who ask him."

From Matthew 7:7–8, 11

Contents

PRAISING GOD   6

DOING GOD'S WILL   14

TRUSTING   28

SEEKING FORGIVENESS   36

SEEKING GOD'S PROTECTION   44

ASKING FOR GOD'S BLESSING   54

INDEX OF FIRST LINES   62

Praising God

Our Father in heaven:
May your holy name be honoured.

MATTHEW 6:9

Our Lord and God! You are worthy
to receive glory, honour, and power.
For you created all things,
and by your will they were given existence
and life.

REVELATION 4:11

White are the wavetops,
White is the snow:
Great is the One
Who made all things below.

Green are the grasslands,
Green is the tree:
Great is the One
Who has made you and me.

Blue are the cornflowers,
Blue is the sky:
Great is the One
Who made all things on high.

Gold is the harvest,
Gold is the sun:
God is our Maker –
Great is the One.

A PSALM OF PRAISE

Praise the Lord from heaven,
all beings of the height!
Praise him, holy angels
and golden sun so bright.

Praise him, silver moonlight,
praise him, every star!
Let your praises shine
throughout the universe so far.

Praise the Lord from earth below,
all beings of the deep!
Lightning, flash! You thunder, roar!
You ocean creatures, leap.

Praise him, hill and mountain!
Praise him, seed and tree.
Praise him, all you creatures
that run the wide world free.

Let the mighty praise him.
Let the children sing.
Men and women, young and old:
Praise your God and king.

FROM PSALM 148

GREAT AND SMALL

All things bright and beautiful,
All creatures great and small,
All things wise and wonderful,
The Lord God made them all.

MRS C. F. ALEXANDER (1818–95)

O God,
Your glory is seen in the sunrise.
O God,
Your glory is seen in the moonrise.
O God,
Your glory is seen in the starshine.
O God,
Your glory is seen in the heavens.

BASED ON PSALM 19

Dear God,
Thank you for the earth that holds us up,
and gravity that holds us down.

For flowers that bloom about our feet,
Father, we thank Thee.
For tender grass so fresh and sweet,
Father, we thank Thee.
For the song of bird and hum of bee,
For all things fair we hear or see,
Father in heaven, we thank Thee.

AUTHOR UNKNOWN

Words and Deeds

Sing to God with thankfulness,
sing a song of praise,
sing out loud and joyfully,
sing out all your days.

FROM PSALM 95

Praise the Lord with trumpets –
all praise to him belongs;
praise him with your music,
your dancing and your songs!

BASED ON PSALM 150

Holy is the Lord my God
and holy are his ways
and holy is the life that I will lead
to give him praise.

MARY JOSLIN

I praise the Lord with all my soul,
my strength, my heart, my mind:
he blesses me with love and grace
and is for ever kind.

BASED ON PSALM 103:1–4

13

Doing God's Will

May your Kingdom come;
may your will be done on earth as it is
  in heaven.

MATTHEW 6:10

Teach me, O God,
to do what is just,
to show constant love
and to live in fellowship with you.

BASED ON MICAH 6:8

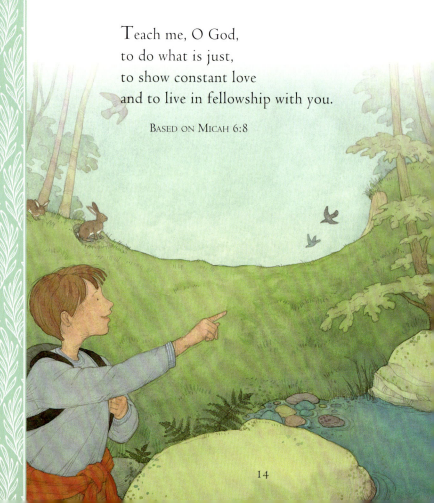

O God, help me not to trust the advice of
wicked people,
but to obey your word in all I do.

For the wicked are nothing more than wisps of
straw in the autumn gale;

But those who obey you and do what is right
are like trees that grow by the river: bearing
leaves, blossom, and a harvest of good fruit.

BASED ON PSALM 1

A LIFE WELL LIVED

O Lord, your word is a lamp to guide me
and a light for my path.

PSALM 119:105

Teach us, Lord,
to serve you as you deserve,
to give and not to count the cost,
to fight and not to heed the wounds,
to toil and not to seek for rest,
to labour and not to ask for any reward
save that of knowing that we do your will.

ST IGNATIUS LOYOLA (1491–1556)

Day by day,
dear Lord, of thee
three things I pray:
to see thee more clearly,
love thee more dearly,
follow thee more nearly,
day by day.

RICHARD, BISHOP OF CHICHESTER (1197–1253)

RESPECT FOR OTHERS

May we learn to appreciate different points
of view:

to know that the view from the hill is different
    from the view in the valley;
the view to the east is different from the view
    to the west;
the view in the morning is different from the
    view in the evening;
the view of a parent is different from the view
    of a child;
the view of a friend is different from the view
    of a stranger;
the view of humankind is different from the
    view of God.

May we all learn to see what is good, what is
true, what is worthwhile.

O God, help us not to despise or oppose what
we do not understand.

WILLIAM PENN (1644–1718)

God said this to the people of Israel:

"Do not ill-treat foreigners who are living in your land. Treat them as you would one of your own people, and love them as you love yourselves. Remember that you were once foreigners in the land of Egypt."

FROM LEVITICUS 19:33–34

LOVE

Lord, make me an instrument of your peace.
Where there is hatred, let me sow love;
Where there is injury, pardon;
Where there is discord, union;
Where there is doubt, faith;
Where there is despair, hope;
Where there is darkness, light;
Where there is sadness, joy.

A PRAYER ASSOCIATED WITH
ST FRANCIS OF ASSISI (C. 1181–1226)

To faith, let me add goodness;
to goodness, let me add knowledge;
to knowledge, let me add self-control;
to self-control, let me add endurance;
to endurance, let me add godliness;
to godliness, let me add affection for my
    brothers and sisters;
to affection, let me add love.

FROM 2 PETER 1:5–7

Jesus said:

"Love one another. As I have loved you, so you must love one another."

JOHN 13:34–35

21

COMMUNITY

Dear God,
Make me good
so I can be a blessing to others.

BASED ON PROVERBS 10:7

Dear God,
When I see someone in trouble,
may I know when to stop and help
and when to hurry to fetch help;
but may I never pass by,
pretending I did not see.

BASED ON JESUS' PARABLE OF THE
GOOD SAMARITAN, LUKE 10:25–37

O God,
Make me more mindful of all those who
support my life and my wellbeing.

Help me to notice the daily acts of kindness
done by friends and strangers alike.

Help me to remember the hours of work that
people do so that I can enjoy food, water, heat,
and light whenever I need it.

Help me to remember those who keep on
working when I can take my leisure.

And when I am asleep, O God, bless and
strengthen those who keep on working.

MARY JOSLIN

PEACE AND JUSTICE

Dear God,
When everything is going wrong I sometimes
wonder why you let bad things happen.

But then you open my eyes to the majesty of
your world, and I know once more that you
are far greater than I can imagine, and I believe
once more that your love and goodness will
not be overcome.

BASED ON THE BOOK OF JOB

Dear God,
We pray for the casualties of war:

for the young and the old,
for the parents and the children;

for the birds and the animals,
for the fields and the flowers;

for the earth and the water,
for the sea and the sky.

We pray for their healing.

Lord, watch over refugees,
their tired feet aching.
Help them bear their heavy loads,
their sore backs breaking.
May they find a place of rest,
no fears awake them.
May you always be their guide,
never forsake them.

Lord, help those who plant and sow,
weed and water, rake and hoe,
toiling in the summer heat
for the food they need to eat.

Bless the work of their tired hands:
turn the dry and dusty land
to a garden, green and gold,
as the harvest crops unfold.

GOD'S KINGDOM

The kingdom of God
is like a tree
growing through all eternity.

It its branches, birds may nest;
in its shade we all may rest.

BASED ON MATTHEW 13:31–32

Dear God,
Help me to find the right way to your
    kingdom,
even though the gate to it be narrow,
and the path difficult to walk.

BASED ON MATTHEW 7:13

Heavenly Father,
may your kingdom come:
may those who have forgotten you remember
    your love;
may those who are trapped in wrongdoing
    believe in your forgiveness;
may those who have lost their way know your
    guiding;
and so may there be joy in heaven today.

BASED ON MATTHEW 6:9–13

Trusting

Give us today the food we need.

MATTHEW 6:11

The bread is warm and fresh,
The water cool and clear.
Lord of all life, be with us,
Lord of all life, be near.

AFRICAN GRACE

The Lord is good to me,
And so I thank the Lord
For giving me the things I need,
The sun, the rain, the appleseed.
The Lord is good to me.

ATTRIBUTED TO JOHN CHAPMAN,
AMERICAN PIONEER AND PLANTER OF ORCHARDS
(1774–1845)

God's Care

Who would make a tiny flower
so beautiful? It lasts an hour!
The bloom then quickly fades away
before the setting of the day.

Who would make a tiny leaf
so intricate? Its life is brief:
a season in the summer sun
before its fluttering life is done.

The One who made both great and small,
who loves and cares for one and all
on land and water, sky and sea:
the One who loves and cares for me.

BASED ON JESUS' SERMON ON THE MOUNT,
MATTHEW 6:25–34

FAMILY AND FRIENDS

I give thanks for the people
who are my home:
we share a place to shelter;
we share our food;
we share our times of work and play and rest.

May we provide one another
with love, encouragement,
respect, and wisdom:
through laughter and celebration,
through tears and troubled times.

May we be to one another
roof and walls,
floor and hearth,
windows and doors.

O God,
We give thanks for the goodhearted people
who love us and do good to us and who show
their mercy and kindness by providing us with
food and drink, house and shelter when we are
in trouble or in need.

FROM A 1739 PRAYER BOOK

Thank you, dear God, for the little place that is my home – more special to me than all the stars in the universe.

ALL GOOD THINGS

Dear God,
Thank you for things I have in abundance,
to enjoy with frivolity.

Thank you for the things of which I have
    enough,
to enjoy thoughtfully.

Thank you that there are things I lack
that keep me trusting in your many blessings.

SOPHIE PIPER

Everyday blessings
include
but are not limited to
sunrise
birdsong
silence
chatter
weeds in flower
doing good for free
a word of praise
daring
surviving
food
the homeward road
an old chair
twilight
stars.

Seeking Forgiveness

Forgive us the wrongs we have done,
as we forgive the wrongs that others have done
to us.

MATTHEW 6:12

God, have mercy on me, a sinner!

THE JESUS PRAYER, FROM LUKE 18:13

I told God everything:
I told God about all the wrong things
I had done.
I gave up trying to pretend.
I gave up trying to hide.
I knew that the only thing to do was
to confess.

And God forgave me.

BASED ON PSALM 32:5

FEELING SORRY

Dear God,
I am not yet ready to say sorry for what I did because I am still trying to pretend that I did not do it.

Dear God,
Please forgive me for saying sorry when I wasn't. Please forgive me for not feeling sorry even now. Please help me untangle my muddled feelings.

Dear God,
For the silly things I have done wrong
I am sorry.

For the serious things I have done wrong
I am sorry.

For the things I didn't even know were wrong
I am sorry.

For all the things I need to put right
Make me strong.

Sophie Piper

Making Amends

Making amends
is an uphill road
and stony is the way.
At the top of the hill
you will find the gate
to a bright new shining day.

Open my eyes
so I can see
the ways I could
more useful be.

Give me the strength
and heart and mind
to do the things
that are good and kind.

May angels guide me through this day;
the paths unknown, but blessed the way.

Sophie Piper

FORGIVING OTHERS

Jesus said:

"If you forgive others the wrongs they have done
to you, your Father in heaven will also forgive you.
But if you do not forgive others, then your Father
will not forgive the wrongs you have done."

MATTHEW 6:14–15

Dear Jesus,
I find it hard to love my enemies.
I do not want to pray for those who are
cruel to me.

I want to follow you, but you are walking
further and faster than I can.
Please come and take me by the hand.

BASED ON MATTHEW 5:43–48

Dear God,
Give us the courage to overcome anger
with love.

Seven
times seven
I freely forgive
and seven
times seventy more.
Lord, give me the grace
to forgive
and forgive,
again
and again
I implore.

BASED ON MATTHEW 18:21–22

43

Seeking God's Protection

Do not bring us to hard testing,
but keep us safe from the Evil One.

<small>MATTHEW 6:13</small>

God is our shelter and strength,
always ready to help in times of trouble.
So we will not be afraid, even if the earth
  is shaken
and mountains fall into the ocean depths;
even if the seas roar and rage,
and the hills are shaken by the violence.

PSALM 46:1–3

LOST

As the rain hides the stars,
as the autumn mist hides the hills,
as the clouds veil the blue of the sky,
so the dark happenings of my lot
hide the shining of your face from me.
Yet, if I may hold your hand in the darkness,
it is enough.
Since I know that,
though I may stumble in my going,
you do not fall.

GAELIC PRAYER (TRANSLATED BY ALISTAIR MACLEAN)

My Lord God, I have no idea where I am going.
I do not see the road ahead of me. I cannot know
for certain where it will end… Therefore I will
trust you always though I may seem to be lost
and in the shadow of death. I will not fear for
you are ever with me, and you will never leave me
to face my perils alone.

ANONYMOUS

Afraid

O God,
I am uncertain.
I am afraid.
My imagination runs wild.
Perhaps the earth will crumble beneath me
and I will fall into endless darkness.

O God,
Keep my feet on holy ground
and choose for me a safe path.

I have been crying in the night, O God;
my pillow is wet with tears.
I am too tired to face the day,
too scared to face those who hate me.

Keep me safe from those evil people;
listen to my cry for help.
Bring all their wickedness to an end;
answer my prayer.

From Psalm 6

In God's strong care

Do not worry,
but in prayer
ask God for what you need
with thankful heart
and simple trust
for God is Lord indeed.

Then peace
far wider than the sky
and deeper than the sea
will fill your heart
and soul and mind
now and eternally.

Based on Philippians 4:6–7

The Lord is my light and my salvation;
I will fear no one.
The Lord protects me from all danger;
I will never be afraid.

PSALM 27:1

MY SHEPHERD GOD

Dear God, you are my shepherd,
You give me all I need,
You take me where the grass grows green
And I can safely feed.

You take me where the water
Is quiet and cool and clear;
And there I rest and know I'm safe
For you are always near.

BASED ON PSALM 23

Loving Shepherd of Thy sheep,
Keep Thy lambs, in safety keep;
Nothing can Thy power withstand;
None can pluck us from Thy hand.

JANE ELIZA LEESON (1807–82)

53

Asking for God's Blessing

May the Lord bless you and take care of you;
May the Lord be kind and gracious to you;
May the Lord look on you with favour and
give you peace.

NUMBERS 6:24–26

One day, when Jesus had finished praying, one of his disciples said to him, "Lord, teach us to pray."

The prayer he gave them is recorded in two Gospels: Matthew 6:9–13 and Luke 11:2–4. Here is a version said today:

Our Father in heaven,
hallowed be your name,
your kingdom come,
your will be done,
on earth as in heaven.
Give us today our daily bread.
Forgive us our sins
as we forgive those who sin against us.
Lead us not into temptation
but deliver us from evil.

THE BEATITUDES

Blessed are the poor in spirit,
  for theirs is the kingdom of heaven.
Blessed are those who mourn,
  for they will be comforted.
Blessed are the meek,
  for they will inherit the earth.
Blessed are those who hunger and thirst for
  righteousness, for they will be filled.

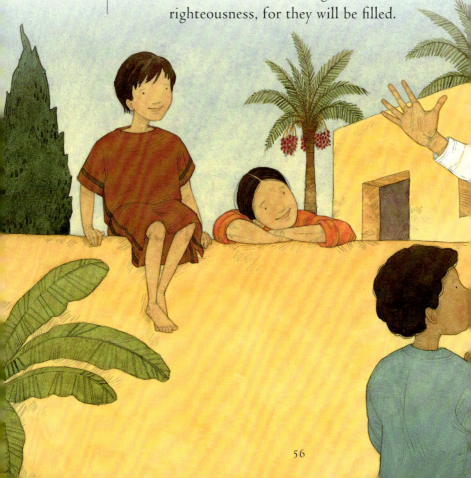

Blessed are the merciful, for they will receive
mercy.
Blessed are the pure in heart, for they will see
God.
Blessed are the peacemakers, for they will be
called children of God.
Blessed are those who are persecuted for
righteousness' sake, for theirs is the
kingdom of heaven.

WORDS OF JESUS FROM MATTHEW 5:3–10

WHEN I LIE DOWN

When I lie down, I go to sleep in peace;
you alone, O Lord, keep me perfectly safe.

PSALM 4:8

God bless all those that I love;
God bless all those that love me;
God bless all those that love those that I love,
And all those that love those that love me.

FROM AN OLD SAMPLER

Lord, send me sleep that I may live;
The wrongs I've done this day forgive.
Bless every deed and thought and word
I've rightly done, or said, or heard.
Bless relatives and friends alway;
Teach all the world to watch and pray.
My thanks for all my blessings take
And hear my prayer for Jesus' sake.

AUTHOR UNKNOWN

Through the Night

Send your peace into my heart, O Lord,
that I may be contented with your mercies
    of this day
and confident of your protection for this
    night;
and having forgiven others,
even as you forgive me,
may I go to my rest in peaceful trust
through Jesus Christ, our Lord, Amen.

St Francis of Assisi (1181–1226)

Deep peace of the running waves to you,
Deep peace of the flowing air to you,
Deep peace of the quiet earth to you,
Deep peace of the shining stars to you,
Deep peace of the shades of night to you,
Moon and stars always giving light to you,
Deep peace of Christ, the Son of Peace,
    to you.

Traditional Gaelic blessing

Index of First Lines

A
All things bright and beautiful   10
As the rain hides the stars   46
"Ask, and you will receive"   4

B
Blessed are the poor in spirit   56

D
Day by day   16
Dear God, For the silly things I have done wrong   39
Dear God, Give us the courage to overcome anger with love   42
Dear God, Help me to find the right way to your kingdom   27
Dear God, I am not yet ready to say sorry   38
Dear God, Make me good   22
Dear God, Please forgive me for saying sorry when I wasn't   38
Dear God, Thank you for the earth that holds us up   10
Dear God, Thank you for things I have in abundance   34
Dear God, We pray for the casualties of war   24
Dear God, When everything is going wrong   24
Dear God, When I see someone in trouble   22
Dear God, you are my shepherd   52

Dear Jesus, I find it hard to love my enemies   42
Deep peace of the running waves to you   60
Do not bring us to hard testing   44
"Do not ill-treat foreigners"   19
Do not worry   50

E
Everyday blessings   35

F
For flowers that bloom about our feet   11
Forgive us the wrongs we have done   56

G
Give us today the food we need   28
God bless all those that I love   58
God is our shelter and strength   45
God, have mercy on me, a sinner   36

H
Heavenly Father, may your kingdom come   27
Holy is the Lord my God   12

I
I give thanks for the people   32
I have been crying in the night, O God   48
I praise the Lord with all my soul   1

I told God everything   36
"If you forgive others the wrongs
    they have done to you"   42

L
Lord, help those who plant and sow
    25
Lord, make me an instrument of your
    peace   20
Lord, send me sleep that I may live
    69
Lord, watch over refugees   25
"Love one another"   21
Loving Shepherd of Thy sheep   53

M
Making amends   40
May angels guide me through this day
    40
May the Lord bless you and take care
    of you   54
May we learn to appreciate different
    points of view   18
May your Kingdom come   14
My Lord God, I have no idea where I
    am going   46

O
O God, help me not to trust the
    advice of wicked people   15
O God, help us not to despise   18
O God, I am uncertain   48
O God, Make me more mindful   23
O God, We give thanks for the
    goodhearted people   32
O God, Your glory is seen in the
    sunrise   10

O Lord, your word is a lamp to guide
    me   16
Open my eyes   40
Our Father in heaven, hallowed be
    your name   55
Our Father in heaven: May your holy
    name be honoured   6
Our Lord and God! You are worthy   6

P
Praise the Lord from heaven   8
Praise the Lord with trumpets   12

S
Send your peace into my heart   60
Seven times seven   43
Sing to God with thankfulness   12

T
Teach me, O God   14
Teach us, Lord   16
Thank you, dear God, for the little
    place that is my home   33
The bread is warm and fresh   28
The kingdom of God   26
The Lord is good to me   28
The Lord is my light and my
    salvation   51
To faith, let me add goodness   20

W
When I lie down, I go to sleep in
    peace   58
White are the wavetops   7
Who would make a tiny flower   30